MW01598965

Acknowledgements

To the individuals who helped make this book possible:

To Dr. Teresa Burns and Eric Hilmer for their fantastic editing.

To Flyover Workshop for their feedback on some of the works contained within.

To Ambrose Ingram, Chelsea Haberkorn, Danielle Hall and Eric Hilmer for being regular and rigorous readers.

To Ambrose Ingram again, for his publishing insights and formatting skills.

To Chelsea Haberkorn again, for her constant companionship and doodles of my other constant companions.

To Eddie Trautner, for his excellent and skilled work creating the cover of this collection.

To you, dear reader, for taking a risk with your money. Art is made by people, and people need to eat

To everyone, thank you. Art is made within communities, and I'm lucky to have found this one.

Previous Appearances

An earlier and less-developed version of *Want and Wanting* first appeared in the 2013 anthology of Aesthetica Magazine. They were the first journal to publish a piece of mine. Check them out.

To Heather

For convincing me to write a happy poem.

Bone Soup

By: Antonio Bouxa

TABLE OF CONTENTS

Consent Agreement

I want to make you sigh, contented,
safe, and to sigh with you, reader.
Together here in this moment, I want
to breathe out all the tension you carry,
let it out of your shoulders, let it out
of your neck and fists. I know
there's a secret spot kept tight, hidden,
full. It is yours to know, reader, but
I want it emptied. I want room in you
for the moment I find the proper words
for copper, for sliver and salt and wire,
for rafter, for preamble, for suture,
for you, for I, for us, so that
there's space to keep them.

Room Temp

I feel it in the gathered collars
in each town that passes identically
through each midwestern window
when I'm traveling between
Wisconsin's icy waters.

In the sullen patrons' feints
at a Midwest friendliness. Vampires
desperate for the warmth of blood
radiating away from other freezing bodies
sheltering from the endless
stretches of fertile earth frozen
until spring.

In the noises of my mother singing
to me at my bedside, I can remember
the scent of spirits warm and oaken.
In our broken farmhouse
and its breathing walls.
The silent snowfall a lonely blanket
here to swallow our little comforts.

In my father's 3 am arrival,
the slush stomped from his worn boots;
the cold breeze storming in with him and
the radiator's denied and leaky efforts.
Fifth-or-handle waterfalls and gentle
humming as his wife unstuck him
from his soggy clothes. Even his kiss
on my cheek was chilling.

We buy our drinks on credit,
its rebellion to give
anything to anyone, to have
anything to give.
There's nothing but poison
wells to drink from to blind us
to the emptiness between them
freezing, with no roadside fires
except the drunken drivers
who've left their wreckage
for us to follow.

Beliefs

I believe in you,
this is not a kindness.
I believe in your capacity
to be acted upon.

I believe in the you I see
on late night sitcom reruns
performing the last lesson
before the signal stops.

I believe broadcast static is
the universe's background radiation,
that the soft hum of absence
is something we can tune in to.

I believe our first apartment was
too small and that every apartment
was too small for two people
living so largely inside themselves.

I believe the static off our tongues
was our warring souls buzzing
bit by bit out of our mouths.
I believe perhaps:

like nuclear reactors,
two isotopes set into containment,
under pressure,
can do nothing but react.

Which is why I believe in
the unharnessed energy;
the violence of our proximity
moves us along,
and no matter our bracings,
we will be moved.

Cat

This poem is about a cat, nothing more.
It is about his paws, and claws, pittering
against the floor's wood, about his bathing
in sun and saliva and how happy he is
when I come home, just as happy as
when I leave. About the food he eats
that he doesn't like that I give to him
because it's healthy and the food that
I give to him because he likes it even
though it isn't healthy and the cage
I keep him in, and how it is large but
still just a cage and how the cage I keep
him in is just a large cage but keeps him
healthy and his life expectancy is longer
than cageless cats but he also expects
so much less than life and such little
living he actually does. It is about cold
nights and warm nights and his finding
warmth everywhere and his pouncing
to share it. It is about his crying when
the bathroom door is shut with him
outside or his crying when the bathroom
door is shut with him inside and its
about his furry flesh and nothing more
and doesn't have to be about anything
because his being, alone, is.

Want and Waiting

It's how the only time
lemmings committed suicide
was when Disney herded thousands
off a cliff and won an award for it.
How we always leave more pennies than we take,
we leave them in the wrong places.
How when we meet someone who doesn't
speak English, we speak English louder.

How when I speak, you speak
Too, and I wish I could run
over your lips; and how sometimes I do.
How belief is our only hammer
for these marble hearts beating
in shallow chests. A single spilt
penny left to weather, to rust beneath
indifferent streetlamps.

How sometimes we'd stare
at moths dancing around those lamps,
and pretend they were UFOs.
How badly we wanted them to be.
How hours after we'd gone to bed
the moths continued dancing.
Tapping against the glass, burning, breathing
bright patterns in the umbrae,
a final binary defiance, in
flicker, flicker, flicker.

I saw a sun in the dark night...

It hung glowing beyond the horizon,
a quiet promise of what is to come.
the first sparks of a funeral pyre
ignited in the whispering night,

soft as the breaths after our fight by the lake
where you told me I was terrible at fishing,
and I told you that I must be okay
because I hooked you.

Or the night you crawled through
the drunken snow like a flightless owl,
asking after someone who could help
you dry your clothes, "who?"

How I dance too close by fire light
and heedless of your warnings, burn
through a dark, silent peace that
I've never learned to navigate, but

in the white noise of your breath
and the softness of your skin like cream,
this darkness recedes.
It is a post-climax clarity.

And just like your swimming
and my fires, and owls hunting
by moonlight and fish chasing
that dangling lure sparkly in the gloam

of the vast empty void we desecrate
with our fighting or the vast empty
void we fill with drunken cries.
All things seek a kinder light.

They strive for stars and sun
and I for celestial you,
your body and your space
and here is a rest;

here is a womb where
filling can be fulfilled by filling and
this truth is the hardest to speak to you,
Starshine.

Confession

What happens when we confess
and it is not enough?
When we've spilled our truths out like spiders,
and instead of cleaning up the buggy ground,
they are stomped on. What good is a story
you don't want to hear? Did I expect
that peace would dawn like the morning,
sky baby blue and novel? No. The only thing
accomplished by confession is a selfish indulgence
that no one needs to know.
There's nothing new to tell you about the
soft curve of your calf,
the briefest touch of your soap,
the way I recognize you by your footfalls.
There's no barricade against time.
No leverage to lift the weight
of the tiny things you hold in your chest
that crack your sternum like a knuckle.
No spoken promise, no soft whispers
of small things in a friendly bed.
There will be no caress as if to say,
"Here I am, we are, and by that
we've made something interminable."
There is no blueprint to continue.

Pulling

I am wondering about
the Mexican restaurant
across from my apartment
in the parking lot.
It has been closed for hours
but I can see inside,
as my car beats
its lights and horn
at the large glass windows.

I am watching for a moment
to offer it an apology,
and let it know I know
what it's like to be full,
and have no one to feed.
To share in its emptiness.

I want to scream alongside the car,
to fill the darkness, the space,
with something more than
an acknowledgement of how empty
many things can be at the same time.

I don't feel the need to stop, yet.
Perhaps tonight, when the car alarm dies
and the lonely siren beats against the dark
canopy, I'll pretend that I, too, am
being broken into, and the prying hands
will pull from me something stereo-like,
a voice.

I'll move to close the window because
I have work in the god-damned morning;
watch shadows slide from the halo
of my overhead lamp and hear
the whine of the dying siren.
And for hours,
watch its fading light
fall back inside.

Bone Soup

I stir the dust of beef bones and spices
into the boiling water. It is 8:20, I'm preparing
for bed. It is supposed to be good for me.
It is supposed to be a good source of protein.
It tastes like the spirit of a meal. It used to be
the way you'd get the last remaining bits
of substance from a thing picked clean.

Roast the bone, break it apart, boil for hours,
it tastes rich and terrible.

It is what you'd have in winter months,
when your hip bones cut your profile;
when the last punky apple is prepared
worm included. It helps you grow old
as old things are supposed to do.

As a child, I'd spread butter
on a large, crusty roll; second dinner.
From the basket by the fridge my
father would keep full.

Perhaps because as a kid,
he'd watch his mother roast bones
and boil them on the stovetop.
Because he was told eating the ants
in the sugar bowl made your eyes pretty.
He kept me full.

Even when I shouldn't have been,
when the doctor recommended
putting away the bread and the butter
and roasting some bones, drinking
some broth. Seeing some winter months.
He encouraged apples.

But every time my grandmother
would poke my ribs,
say I was thin, ask my dad
why I didn't eat more,
we went clothes shopping.

I am stirring dust into water.
I am thinking of all the starving
I never had to do, and I am hearing
the doctor say that, maybe,
starving would be good for me.

Consumption

If I had a pool, I'd drown myself,
but no one has ever paid much
for a reflection
of the way they pick at scabs.

There is no drowning to be done.
So instead I'll eat
an entire fried chicken and throw it back up.
There are many ways to get to the shadows
of risen bruises under your eyes.

Finding something to choke on
is the point of the whole exercise.
But it is important
to stall your breath the right way;
and I am trying.

You told me once, by text,
after I had asked if I could see you
that loneliness was the symptom
of thinking we deserved something.

"What we've done
and what we get,
are an undigested meal."
You can't sift meaning from the bowl.

I miss the you I've never gotten.
I miss the glimpses caught
in the drunk unguarded laugher
and sober secret singing I've
tried recklessly to see again.

I want to digest you,
to consume the you
I've failed to drown myself in,
and to make meaning from it

To find you a space to take your breath,
to drop your shoulders, untuck your belly.
To wield it at you like an idol,
a charm against abandonment.

Thermodynamics

Today is the third day
I've gone without a shower .
The garbage has decided
to demonstrate against these actions.
Row upon row of empty bottles sit,
gutted phylacteries,
their prayers digested and unreadable.
Things do not pass with time
outside the window.

What is it, to be dead, brain?
There are so many micro deaths
available but only a word for one.
There is no drama in the process, only
the process. It is suggested
even the universe terminates.

The phenomenon is called heat death.
The universe runs out of steam,
decides that the sofa's location
is good enough. That it shouldn't sit
while watching T.V. anyway.
It's a cold death.

All deaths are cold, because death
is frictionless, and it's the small ones
that slide slowly away from
the center. Like our cosmos
we will find an edge to stop along.
It's not the fall that kills you.

It's the stop.

Today is the third day
I've gone without a shower,
but before I christen myself
and make an offering
to the pet's empty food bowl,
there is one thing
I have to ask.

Is it still freezing outside?

Café Paraiso Noir

I make a cast
of blood and bone;
of spit and saltwater.
The wine is not sanguine,
they call it *refresco*.

This film opens like a war movie.
We order familiar drinks
in a foreign tongue, strange tobacco
hanging off our lips, a waitress
fumbles English for us.

Men perch on stools
late into the evening, and we
drink by the thimble
what is taken
by the drop.

The discoteca's music echoes
down stone hallways
of the city's heart, where
every good woman knows
we're only looking for a gesture.

The cafés clear and our walk
into the countryside is lonesome.
Feral hounds that strut in packs
abandon unity when observed. Guilty,
disrupting the evening palms' solitude.

The one remaining
sets upon us walking
shoulder to shoulder.
All packs are to dissolve,
and we're hairier than the beasts.

The saltwater is sweet
and sweaty. The wine rises
in my throat a growl,
and a waning moon sets
the lighting for our final scene.

Everyone dies in this movie.

A Forward-Looking Statement

Once discovered,
I will no longer write of birds.
There's nothing to escape
there or anywhere;
nothing in the wind
the dirt cannot offer.

We have only what we wake to.
We've said enough about the rest.

Thermostat

The needle climbed, and, ascending,
you saw and jerked over to the shoulder
while vapor poured from my hood.

You pulled over behind me, eyes streaming
from the weariness and cold pick of February wind.
As I opened up my metal box and tinkered

with the radiator. Did I burn my hand or did you
Stop me? I cannot recall, but the warning dash remained
glowing in the ghost-light of the highway. I pulled

you against the frame and kissed your forehead,
suggested turning off your lights.
You kissed back and insisted:

It would not be long,
we would wait together.
I was angry with you.
I wished to wait alone,

and glow after you
a warning light,
red and envious of the attention
the rest of the night was getting.

County Representatives

They sit round-table Monday morning;
custard eyes, broken blood vessels; keep
the hair around their lips trimmed back.

The hoarse and pallid corn men,
gray skin on gray tables where
pudgy sad women gaze concerned

in their suits and chairs, their
kernelled flesh and ethanol stomachs,
cold hands, poor circulation filling

vast skies as empty as their choked voices.
Drink whisky that burns hot but clear;
the invisible fire in their bellies

far warmer than the dead corn stalking
under dead and frozen clouds, so
they turn to filling with sweet and fat

and spirit, sadly knowing it is
better to die full of something
than to suffer as an empty space.

Gone Clubbing

God's not here yet? I asked, and she said:
There's a waiting line that looks
like the ball dropped in New York
on New Year's Eve, when thousands of tourists
orgify themselves to witness
measured time's descent upon them
because the last rotation wasn't good enough.

My friend said she'd gotten to Times Square
at 8 a.m. one year and could hardly see the ball.
Most people had been waiting since at least 6.
She told me this with her neck craned skyward
in a form to watch for stormy omens.
Someone else who was with her had
to leave early because the cold had
eaten a bit of her favorite fingertip,
and she couldn't stand to lose any more.

The best celebrations, they'll tell you,
happen in obscure clubs and bars
where the locals gather laughing, warm and cradled,
At the strangers trampled by the coming novelty.

Predation

I'm not sure what I am supposed to be making
here on this page, what art I should leave
you, Reader. What paths I'm supposed
to help you navigate when I've walked so few
and even those briefly, I'm not sure:

of my responsibility to make, or to make of;
the first time my father took me hunting,
I shivered clutching a too-large-for-me
shotgun, on a collapsible stool, back against
a tree waiting for a deer that may or may never
come. Or that a few years later I'd be holding

a different gun but walking through the same
wood, with different boys who would shoot
shrews and squirrels because they were bored
and there was nothing bigger. Their father
chuckling as blood and cartilage baptized
the air and dappled the dirt.

I made out with one of those boys' girlfriends,
right after they broke up at a party because
he would fuck her and leave
for hours without talking was their summary.
The first time we went hunting, my father and I,
I saw a golden-brown coyote stalk across the snow
I asked if I could shoot it. He said yes if I wanted to.

When the boys would shoot at field mice, sometimes
I'd look at my father and he'd turn away,
walling himself from the violence, but
we would still hunt with them and more
shrews would die. And when I think about the boy's

girlfriend crying with her tongue in my mouth,
I think about the coyote, and when I think about
the coyote, I think about this writing and I feel
in some ways like my father must have felt
when I asked him if we could kill for sport
because I was bored of killing for food.

Because he didn't know what to say
because we could, and we couldn't, and
on this page, you and I can, and we can't, but,
whatever we do, I don't want any blood
on my hands but my own.

23

Paterfamilias

I remember the way
my head bounced
on your shoulder
up the stairs,
in your arms.
Your god-like
cologne and stubble.
The weird ghosts
that fled from you
in our first farmhouse.
It's this nostalgia
that I'll speak to
when it's your ghost
I'm running from
when the child
in my arms asks
who you were.

Reconstitution

The fumes of your memory
reek, as I burn through
my bedroom closet.
Like June rain through baby's breath.
I wonder how it would be
to free myself from
the journeys of your past;
of the cobblestones
I failed to lay for you.

To dash them like an infant
skull on earth. To hold it
over the edge of what I know
and lose it.
To have you lean over me and say
"otherwise." However,
without the providence of Isaac
we are all weary pilgrims.

Gigil is a word in Fillipino
for the urge to squeeze something
unbearably cute, or sweet.
Language aches still
to sound a description
of madness caused by something
that could make you happy.

I have lied.
In every plan I ever made.
There was never any belief
that things could be
"otherwise."
The ghost of your morning
breath reminds me every time,
that we are remnants
of a desperate corpse.

Kintsugi is a Japanese art form.
Where sculptors hide damaged pasts.
Where history is scoured
and filled with gold.
They know there is nothing beautiful
about all the gold
I've rubbed into our story.
No matter how long you stare at
the sparkles, the patterned fractures
map out the tale.

Desenrascanço doesn't mean to bullshit,
in Portuguese, it means
to bullshit fantastically.
It means to cobble the truth
together from the bones
of reality you have at hand, and
that's what I've been doing.
Cutting my hands grasping
at the edges of a leftover truth

Zero Sum

We've come this far.
Let's go a little further
Reader, you've stuck by
me for so long
I can't pretend now.

        The little things that stick so well to us;
        claw sheaths, cancer, compositions
        captured on the tongues of toddlers
        and tarot cards and to ponder
        that all those who wander wonder
        what's to follow, you follow? Is it you?

                Here it meanders, like the
                stalking housecat or murdered
                bird—this is the place to line
                and die and be borne again
                like Nobakov and fire
                and the sun.

As concrete as the roads
we took to get here.
As real
as the body count.

        I was writing you a song
        when the clock skipped
        and I had too many words
        for the time left.

                We are always close to it,
                the little death, cat perched on
                baby's chest purring at the purring
                desperate airy gasps.

        So many slips come in threes
        Father, Son, and Holy Spirit
        Christ, cradle, clay.

Reader, did you know
Grover warned every child
long before they could read
that something is hidden
at the end of this book?

        Dreidel, dreidel, dreidel,   27
        together we will play.

                                        Each conversation is
                                  a forward-looking bargain;
                                     an unfair assumption.

There are miracles, Reader.
You are one of them.
But miracles come often,
in the form of lessons.

                        Nun, Gimmel, Hey, Shin,
                              to turn and turn,
                              and turn and turn.
                        To learn, the empty side
                        is too often the heaviest.

                                  But I'll agree to look forward
                                                       even if
                                              I'm no longer sure
                                        what to look forward to.

                  As empty as the air shimmering
                     off the ember of the joint
                     death-gripped by your teeth
                  as you dance. A pale-assed oracle.

I've never learned
the difference in
learning from and
taking from.

                  You turn and turn, and I
                  turn you over and over in
                  my head for every last thing
                  I can take from you

                                        It's been this way for a while.
                                        It's been this way before
                                        enough that I could bet
                                             on the ending.

I swear to you, Reader:
all free lessons are worth-
less. I swear: I'd bite you
if I had the teeth for it.

                  Or anyone really.
                  For anyone counting
               the miles of bodies walked,
            the flesh crossed for fulfillment
                  wasn't enough.   28

But it's your flesh, Reader,
that makes chewing worth the effort,
the beauty in the bricks of your street
that makes walking them to rubble worthwhile.

The truth is thus,
each rapture, each rupture,
each peaceful revolt against
the bystanders, was glorious.

It is probably why every holy book
ends in the death, of the self, or of
the world; if to rest is promised:
this burden has an expiration date.

Maybe it's your morning-after hair,
the headlights of your nipples through
fabric, the stains of your memory
or the memory of stains on your fabric.

Reader, whatever it is, it is
what we will hold on to,
termination is the only thing
our tiny minds can frame.

Before the end,
I want to apologize
for my face buried in snow,
the words buried in your throat,
the things I won't allow you to say.

I am so very sorry
about all you had to give
that I could take so very long
to learn so very little.

About the Author

Antonio Bouxa is an alumnus of the University of Wisconsin – Platteville where he obtained a bachelor's degree in Philosophy and Professional writing. By day he is a business operations consultant specializing in stakeholder management. By night he is an author, tabletop gamemaster and cat dad. He currently resides in Madison, Wisconsin.

CPSIA information can be obtained
at www.ICGtesting.com
Printed in the USA
LVHW111506220120
644433LV00001B/136